Best Easy Day Hikes Series

Best Easy Day Hikes
Grand Rapids
Michigan

Kevin Revolinski

FALCONGUIDES

GUILFORD, CONNECTICUT
HELENA, MONTANA

AN IMPRINT OF GLOBE PEQUOT PRESS

FALCONGUIDES®

Copyright © 2012 Morris Book Publishing, LLC

FalconGuides is an imprint of Globe Pequot Press.
Falcon, FalconGuides, and Outfit Your Mind are registered trademarks
of Morris Book Publishing, LLC.

Project editor: David Legere
Layout: Joanna Beyer
Maps created by Alena Pearce © Morris Book Publishing, LLC

TOPO! Explorer software and SuperQuad source maps courtesy of
National Geographic Maps. For information about TOPO! Explorer,
TOPO!, and Nat Geo Maps products, go to www.topo.com or www
.natgeomaps.com.

Library of Congress Cataloging-in-Publication Data is available on file.

ISBN 978-0-7627-7245-2

Printed in the United States of America

10 9 8 7 6 5 4 3 2 1

Contents

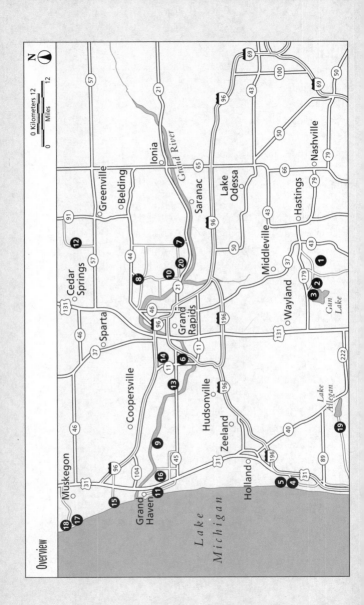

Overview

Lake Michigan

N

0 Kilometers 12
0 Miles 12

Muskegon
Grand Haven
Cedar Springs
Sparta
Coopersville
Greenville
Belding
Ionia
Saranac
Lake Odessa
Grand Rapids
Hudsonville
Zeeland
Holland
Middleville
Wayland
Hastings
Nashville
Lake Allegan
Gun Lake
Grand River

31
57
91
131
46
37
57
44
21
65
46
96
11
104
45
96
31
40
89
222
131
37
179
43
37
50
96
43
66
79
79
50
100
69
69
50

18 17
15
16
11
5 4
19
9
13
14
6
8
10 20
12
7
1
2
3

Acknowledgments

Behind every author is the collection of great people who showed him or her the way. Thanks to Charlie Conley at DeLorme for bringing me over to a great GPS product that made mapping easier than ever. (Also recommended to me by colleague and outdoor hero, Johnny Molloy.) Here's a shout-out for P. J. Hoffmaster State Park, which served as base camp while I researched this book. I am grateful to Bruce Matthews for his help and a trail drop for the North Country Trail. A huge thanks to Dave Lorenz at Travel Michigan for a lot of great advice and connecting me to the right people. And, of course, thanks to all the people who work behind the scenes, in parks or in politics, to create, protect, and maintain the wonderful park system of the state of Michigan. It's a treasure for all.

Introduction

Grand Rapids is an interesting place from a hiker's perspective. While it has a few good natural places, such as Millennium Park and the magnificent Blandsford Nature Center, it is also surrounded by an evenly distributed collection of state and county parks. Along the network of highways and interstates that head in all directions from the city, you can get off at an exit and find a well preserved bit of wilderness to disappear into. The North Country National Scenic Trail—at over 4,600 miles through seven states, the longest of the national trails—is just a short drive away. Getting out of the city is a snap and a hike doesn't need a lot of preplanning because you never have far to drive. And then there's the proximity of Lake Michigan.

For much of my life just across the lake in Wisconsin, I had heard about the dunes of Michigan, something that as a child I had associated with deserts or at least seaside shores. They always had a mystical quality for me, and when I finally had the opportunity to see them and hike them, I was not disappointed. In fact, beyond the natural beauty of them is the geological history they imply. They are reminders of Nature painting a story with a very large brush. Glaciers, over a mile thick in places, carved out these Great Lakes and left behind the waters and the sands that were blown into massive drifts. What's left behind—both the exposed sands and those reclaimed by forests and grasses along their ridged backs—is startling and beautiful, and the views of the lakes from the state parks are breathtaking.

But while those dunes might receive top billing for this show, the parks and trails farther inland deserve a lot of

appreciation as well. Charming creeks through pine forests, a well developed system of county parks, rugged recreation areas set aside for wildlife—all of them have something different to offer from the next park down the road.

Otis Sanctuary gets the nod from Audubon as being a prime birding site, with a great combination of habitats in a small area, something you can find not just here but at other parks such as Yankee Springs or Pickerel Lake. The North Country Trail is rugged and less parklike. It crosses the state, often just steps from developed land but somehow sneaking by in a preserved sense of the wild thanks to cooperative landowners, the National Park System, and all the volunteers and donors who made it possible. Yankee Springs has a huge system of trails and, like the dunes, exhibits evidence of that larger ice age story.

The characters of each hike in this book vary, and in each of these state, county, and city parks, I have put together a route that captures the essence of that particular park. But these are merely suggestions on where to start. Most of these trails have alternatives or are part of a larger system. You may find that some corners of a park might compel you to linger a bit longer and explore spur trails or other loops. Whatever you choose, my hope is that you enjoy the rich natural beauty of this little corner of Michigan.

The Nature of Grand Rapids

Grand Rapids' hiking grounds range from the rugged and hilly to the flat and paved. Hikes in this guide cover the gamut. While by definition a best easy day hike is not strenuous and generally poses little danger to the traveler, knowing a few details about the nature of the Grand Rapids area will enhance your explorations.

Weather

Spring can start in March or May, depending on the whims of Michigan weather. But in general you can expect temperatures to get above freezing in March and stay there by April. Temperatures in the 50s, 60s, and even 70s can be expected in April and May. Mosquitoes start coming out later in May or, if you're lucky, June.

Summer temperatures can range from the 60s and 70s in June up to the 80s and 90s in July and August. But don't be surprised by 85 one day and 65 the next day—or even a couple of hours later. Mosquitoes and summer go hand in hand, I'm afraid. Watch for thunderstorms or the occasional windstorm or tornado.

Fall brings amazing colors starting in late September and perhaps hanging on past Halloween. Some 70s and 80s heat can linger through September, but generally temperatures are mild and the mosquitoes have gone for the year.

Winter means snow. This does not, however, mean the end of the hiking season. Most trails are still open in the winter, and snowshoe enthusiasts can be happy. However, watch for trails that are closed to hikers when cross-country skiing is possible. Groomed trails as a rule prohibit hiking.

Critters

There's not much in the way of dangerous wildlife. Just don't find yourself on the business end of a skunk. You'll encounter mostly benign, sweet creatures on these trails, such as deer, squirrels, rabbits, wild turkeys, and a variety of songbirds and shorebirds. More rarely seen (during the daylight hours especially) are coyotes, raccoons, and opossums. Deer in some of the parks are remarkably tame, and may linger on or close to the trail as you approach.

The only real critter risks come from the smallest of the lot: the mosquito and the tick, which can carry West Nile virus and Lyme disease, respectively. Protect yourself with light-colored clothing and good insect repellent, and check yourself for ticks after every hike.

Safety and Preparation

Hiking in the Grand Rapids area is generally safe. Still, hikers should be prepared, whether they are out for a short stroll through Millennium Park or working up and down the dunes along Lake Michigan's shores. Some specific advice:

- Know the basics of first aid, including how to treat bleeding, bites and stings, and fractures, strains, or sprains. Pack a first-aid kit on each excursion.

- Use maps to navigate (and do not rely solely on the maps included in this book).

- Bring or wear clothes to protect you from cold, heat, or rain.

- Familiarize yourself with the symptoms of heat exhaustion, heat stroke, and hypothermia. Heat exhaustion symptoms include heavy sweating, muscle cramps, headache, dizziness, and fainting. Should you or any of your hiking party exhibit any of these symptoms, cool the victim down immediately by rehydrating and getting him or her to an air-conditioned location. Cold showers also help reduce body temperature. Heat stroke is much more serious: The victim may lose consciousness, and the skin is hot and dry to the touch. In this event, call 911 immediately. Heat stroke is a real possibility, especially on a hot summer day at the exposed dunes.

Hypothermia doesn't require extremely cold temperatures—even prolonged exposure can gradually lower your core body temperature, and getting wet can exacerbate that quickly. Symptoms include shivering, clumsiness or lack of coordination, slurred speech, drowsiness, confusion and poor decision making (such as trying to remove warm clothes), and in extreme cases, progressive loss of consciousness, weak pulse, and slow, shallow breathing. If you or a fellow hiker exhibit signs of hypothermia, get to shelter or a warm place, remove wet clothing, and put on layers of clothes or blankets. Seek medical attention as soon as possible.

- Regardless of the weather, your body needs a lot of water while hiking. A full 32-ounce bottle is the minimum for these short hikes, but more is always better. Bring a full water bottle, whether water is available along the trail or not.

- Don't drink from streams, rivers, creeks, or lakes without treating or filtering the water first. Waterways and water bodies may host a variety of contaminants, including giardia, which can cause serious intestinal unrest.

- Prepare for extremes of both heat and cold by dressing in layers.

- Carry a backpack in which you can store extra clothing, ample drinking water and food, and whatever goodies, like guidebooks, cameras, and binoculars, you might want.

- Some area trails have cell phone coverage. Bring your device, but make sure you've turned it off or got it on

the vibrate setting while hiking. Nothing like a "wake the dead"–loud ring to startle every creature, including fellow hikers.

- Keep children under careful watch. Hazards along some of the trails include poison ivy and poison oak, uneven footing, deep water, and steep drop-offs; make sure children don't stray from the designated route. Children should carry a plastic whistle; if they become lost, they should stay in one place and blow the whistle to summon help.

Leave No Trace

Trails in the Grand Rapids area are heavily used year-round. We, as trail users and advocates, must be especially vigilant to make sure our passage leaves no lasting mark. Here are some basic guidelines for preserving trails in the region:

- Avoid damaging trailside soils and plants by remaining on the established route. This is also a good rule of thumb for avoiding trailside irritants, like poison ivy.
- Pack out all your own trash, including biodegradable items like orange peels. You might also pack out garbage left by less considerate hikers. Use outhouses at trailheads or along the trail, and keep water sources clean.
- Don't pick wildflowers or gather rocks, antlers, feathers, and other treasures along the trail. Removing these items will only take away from the next hiker's experience.
- Be careful with fire. Use a camp stove for cooking. Be sure it's OK to build a campfire in the area you're visiting. Use an existing fire ring and keep your fire small.

Use sticks from the ground as kindling. Burn all the wood to ash and be sure the fire is completely out and cold before leaving.

- Don't approach or feed any wild creatures—the ground squirrel eyeing your snack food is best able to survive if it remains self-reliant. Control pets at all times.

- Be kind to other visitors. Be courteous by not making loud noises while hiking and be aware that you share the trail with others. Yield to other trail users when appropriate.

For more information, visit www.lnt.org.

Wilderness Regulations

You will find the lands listed in this book both accessible and fairly easy to navigate. Only the state parks charge admission fees.

While most of the parks have picnic areas with trash receptacles, some of the parks, forests, and preserves are "carry-in, carry-out" areas. This means that you must take all of your trash with you for disposal outside the park.

Some preserves do not permit pets, and in all cases where they are allowed, dogs and other pets must be leashed. You will see dogs running free in some parks, but park regulations and county leash laws prohibit this. It's also illegal to leave your dog's droppings in parks; you can face fines for not cleaning up after your pet.

If you're a gun owner, you will need to leave your weapon at home when entering a county park, as only law enforcement officers are permitted to carry guns on these lands. Hunting is permitted in some properties managed by the Department of Natural Resources, so it's a good idea

to wear an orange jacket and hat if you're planning to hike these areas during hunting seasons.

Land Management

The following government and private organizations manage most of the public lands described in this guide, and can provide further information on these hikes and other trails in their service areas:

- Michigan Department of Natural Resources, Mason Building, Sixth Floor, PO Box 30028, Lansing MI 48909; (517) 373-9900; www.michigan.gov/dnr. A complete listing of state parks is available on the website, along with park brochures and maps.

- Grand Rapids Parks & Recreation, 201 Market Ave. SW, Grand Rapids, MI 49503; (616) 456-3232; www.grcity.us/11248. The park office is open Mon through Fri, 7:30 a.m. to 4:30 p.m.

- Kent County Parks, 1700 Butterworth St. SW, Grand Rapids, MI 49534-7065; (616) 336-PARK (7275); www.accesskent.com/CultureLeisureAndTransit/Parks.

A portion of the North Country National Scenic Trail is included in this book. For more information about this national trail, contact the North Country Trail Association, 229 East Main St., Lowell, MI 49331; (866) 445-3628; www.northcountrytrail.org. This 2,800-member club works together to maintain and sometimes develop segments for the North Country Trail. Watch for group hikes and other activities.

Public Transportation

Grand Rapids has a great public transit system known as The Rapid, which offers fixed-route bus service throughout the Grand Rapids metropolitan area. Contact the administrative offices for more information at 300 Ellsworth Ave. SW, Grand Rapids, MI 49503-4005 or (616) 456-7514. The office is open weekdays from 8 a.m. to 4:30 p.m. There is a system map on the website at www.ridetherapid.org.

How to Use This Guide

This guide is designed to be simple and easy to use. The overview map at the beginning of the book shows the location of each hike by number, keyed to the table of contents. Each hike is accompanied by a route map that shows access roads, the highlighted featured route, and directional arrows to point you in the right direction. It indicates the general outline of the hike, but due to scale restrictions, is not as detailed as a park map might be or even as the Miles and Directions are. While most of the hikes are on clearly designated paths, use these route maps in conjunction with other resources.

Each hike begins with summary information that delivers the trail's vital statistics, including length, difficulty, fees and permits, park hours, canine compatibility, and trail contacts. Directions to the trailhead are also provided, along with a general description of what you'll see along the way. A detailed route finder (Miles and Directions) sets forth mileages between significant landmarks along the trail.

Hike Selection

This guide describes trails that are accessible to every hiker, whether a visitor from out of town or someone lucky enough to live in the Grand Rapids area. The hikes are no longer than 7 miles round-trip, and some are considerably shorter. They range in difficulty from flat excursions perfect for a family outing to more challenging treks in the dunes along Lake Michigan's shores. While these trails are among the best, keep in mind that nearby trails, often in the same park or preserve, may offer options better suited to your needs. I've sought to space hikes evenly in and around Grand

Rapids, so wherever your starting point, you'll find a great easy day hike nearby.

Difficulty Ratings

These are all easy hikes, but easy is a relative term. Some would argue that no hike involving any kind of climbing is easy, and certainly any hike with sand dunes is going to require a bit more effort. To aid in the selection of a hike that suits particular needs and abilities, each is rated easy, moderate, or more challenging. Bear in mind that most challenging routes can be made easy by hiking within your limits and taking rests when you need them.

- **Easy** hikes are generally short and flat, taking no longer than 1.5 to 2 hours to complete.

- **Moderate** hikes involve increased distance and relatively mild changes in elevation, and will take about 3 hours to complete.

These are completely subjective ratings—consider that what you think is easy is entirely dependent on your level of fitness and the adequacy of your gear (primarily shoes). If you are hiking with a group, you should select a hike with a rating that's appropriate for the least fit and prepared in your party.

Approximate hiking times are based on the assumption that on flat ground, most walkers average 2 miles per hour. Adjust that rate by the steepness of the terrain and your level of fitness (subtract time if you're an aerobic animal or add time if you're hiking with kids), and you have a ballpark hiking duration. Be sure to add more time if you plan to picnic or take part in other activities like bird watching or photography.

Trail Finder

Best Hikes for River Lovers

Best Hikes for Lake Lovers

Best Hikes for Sand Dunes

Best Hikes for Children

Best Hikes for Dogs

Best Hikes for Great Views

Best Hikes for Nature Lovers

Map Legend

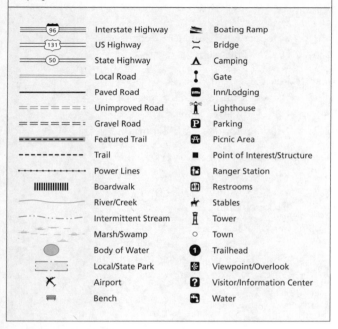

96	Interstate Highway	Boating Ramp
131	US Highway	Bridge
50	State Highway	Camping
	Local Road	Gate
	Paved Road	Inn/Lodging
	Unimproved Road	Lighthouse
	Gravel Road	Parking
	Featured Trail	Picnic Area
	Trail	Point of Interest/Structure
	Power Lines	Ranger Station
	Boardwalk	Restrooms
	River/Creek	Stables
	Intermittent Stream	Tower
	Marsh/Swamp	Town
	Body of Water	Trailhead
	Local/State Park	Viewpoint/Overlook
	Airport	Visitor/Information Center
	Bench	Water

1 Otis Sanctuary

With a bit of wetlands, hardwood forest, and open prairie, this Audubon sanctuary makes an easy hike and offers a variety of resident and migratory bird species.

Distance: 1.9-mile lollipop
Hiking time: About 1 hour
Difficulty: Easy
Trail surface: Grass, some packed dirt
Best season: Year-round
Other trail users: None
Canine compatibility: Dogs not permitted
Fees and permits: None
Schedule: Open daily dawn to dusk
Maps: TOPO! CD: Eastern Region 4; USGS Cloverdale; maps at map board

Trail contact: Michigan Audubon Society, Otis Sanctuary, 3560 Havens Rd., Hastings, MI 49058; (269) 948-5777; www.michigan audubon.org
Special considerations: While open in winter, the road is only plowed to the resident manager's house, not the lot, so parking is on the road at that time.
Other: Stop in the office for a map and information about local birding events.

Finding the trailhead: From MI 179 take MI 43 south 2.9 miles to Goodwill Road. Turn right (west) and go 1.7 miles to Havens Road. Take this left (south) 0.6 mile to the parking lot on the right, past the farmhouse. The trailhead is at the southeastern corner of the lot. GPS: N42 36.0481' / W85 23.4349'

The Hike

While this is an Audubon Society sanctuary and you can expect a good variety of birds—including Henslow's sparrow, if you are lucky—there is also a chance you might see a

rattlesnake. Keep your eyes open both for the opportunity to see a rare creature and to avoid meeting one more personally.

Starting from the parking lot, cross the road to enter the eastern portion of the sanctuary on a wide mowed path. You will find a map board here and some laminated maps that you must return at the end of the hike. Just 500 feet along, the trail splits. Your return path is to the left; you hike to the right. Another 150 feet brings you to a spur trail that leads to a clearing with a cabin that has restrooms (which are not always open—use the portable toilet at the parking lot), a picnic table, and a swing set.

The trail curls uphill then among spruce, and at the top of the hill you enter into a wide field and pass a short spur trail to a bench. Watch for benches along the route to sit and admire the views or wait for birds. The next bench at 0.3 mile offers a sweeping view of the field and forest beyond. At 0.5 mile enter the woods on a packed dirt trail with a scattering of acorns. Within the woods is a pond that attracts wildlife but has also choked off a few trees. A bench overlooks it. You reach a map board at 0.7 mile, which is an alternative exit and parking area on Hull Road and the midpoint of this loop. Stay left to skip the spur to the exit.

In another 600 feet you pass through alpine plantation, then the trail heads back uphill through a field with scattered brush. Grasses are quite tall in summer, and as you get closer to the trail you came in on, the brush thickens, though you can still see the park's barn. Once back out on the road, walk back to the barn and stroll the boardwalk out to the edge of the marsh. There is a bench there as well. Backtrack to your car when you are ready to leave.

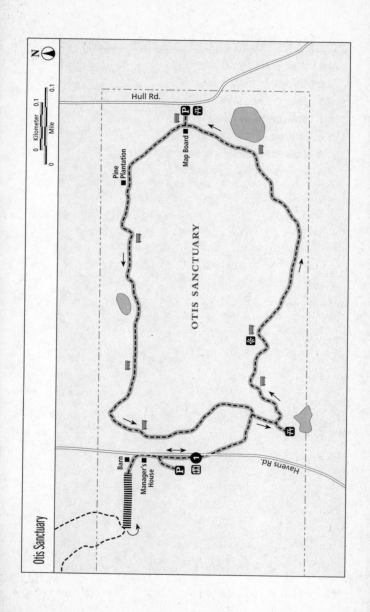

Otis Sanctuary

N

OTIS SANCTUARY

Pine Plantation

Map Board

Hull Rd.

Barn

Manager's House

Havens Rd.

0 Kilometer 0.1
0 Mile 0.1

Miles and Directions

0.0   Start from the trailhead.

0.1   Go right at the first juncture.

0.5   Enter the woods.

0.7   Pass the map board.

1.4   Return to Havens Road.

1.6   Enter the boardwalk to the marsh.

1.9   Arrive back at the parking lot.

2 Yankee Springs Recreation Area– Hall Lake Trail

Tucked among ridges and some boggy areas, the trail starts in rich forest and, after an impressive climb of a scenic hill, takes you along a lovely lakeshore.

Distance: 1.9-mile loop
Hiking time: About 1 hour
Difficulty: Moderate due to some low-grade climbs
Trail surface: Packed dirt
Best season: Spring, summer, fall
Other trail users: Cross-country skiers
Canine compatibility: Dogs permitted on a 6-foot leash
Fees and permits: Michigan State Park Motor Vehicle Permit required for entry
Schedule: Open daily 4 a.m. to 11 p.m.

Maps: TOPO! CD: Eastern Region 4; USGS Cloverdale; maps at the park office and trailhead
Trail contact: Yankee Springs Recreation Area, 2104 South Briggs Rd., Middleville, MI 49333; (269) 795-9081; www .dnr.state.mi.us
Special considerations: No facilities along the trail or near the trailhead. Maps are in a map box (sometimes) at the trailhead, and there is a self-pay box for the park fee.
Other: This park participates in the Michigan State Park Outdoor Explorer Program.

Finding the trailhead: Drive south on US 131 to exit 61 for MI 179. At the exit, turn left onto 12th Street for under 0.1 mile to reach MI 179, where you turn left (east). Go east 7.7 miles and follow the curve to the right (south) at Briggs Road. Briggs becomes Gun Lake Road, and from MI 179 it's a total distance of 2 miles to find the park entrance on the left (north). The trailhead is right there as you enter the park. GPS: N42 36.819' / W85 29.396'

The Hike

About a third of this hike is along the scenic shore of Hall Lake. The walk is gentle at first but a bit more vigorous as it passes between ridges and ultimately climbs Graves Hill. To extend the hike, consider continuing on to the Devil's Soup Bowl.

The trail splits just inside the woods, and you go left through mixed forest. Be aware that cross-country ski trails cross the path from time to time. Stay on the marked trail. At 0.3 mile you'll pass under power lines and see a pond to your right. At 0.7 mile the North Country Trail and Long Lake Trail join from the left, and all overlap on this segment up to Graves Hill. A T juncture at 0.9 mile offers a spur trail to the left. This will take you 300 feet up to the overlook (which isn't much of an overlook when the foliage of summer is in). You can add another 0.6 mile of out-and-back by continuing over the hill on a challenging trail to see the Devil's Soup Bowl, a scenic overlook into a deep kettle formation made by the glaciers of old.

Trace your steps back to that juncture below Graves Hill and continue on the loop. Hall Lake becomes visible to the left as the trail gradually comes alongside the water. Outside of the optional spur trail to Devil's Soup Bowl, the lake is the highlight of this hike. Eventually you cross a footbridge, and just past that you'll see that the North Country Trail continues along the lakeshore to the south. At this juncture the Hall Lake Trail goes right (west), taking you back through the forest to the trailhead.

Miles and Directions

0.0 Start from the trailhead.

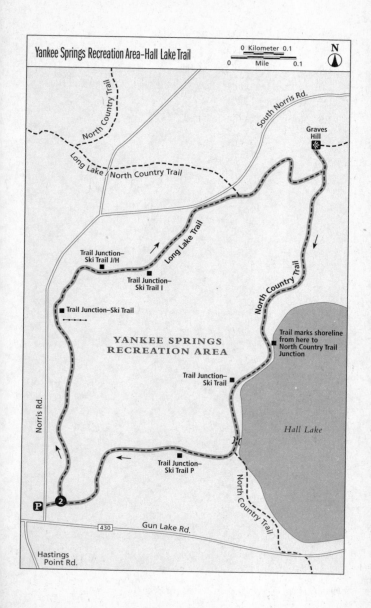

Yankee Springs Recreation Area–Hall Lake Trail

0 Kilometer 0.1

0 Mile 0.1

N

North Country Trail

Long Lake / North Country Trail

South Norris Rd.

Graves Hill

Long Lake Trail

Trail Junction–Ski Trail J/H

Trail Junction–Ski Trail I

Trail Junction–Ski Trail

North Country Trail

Trail marks shoreline from here to North Country Trail Junction

YANKEE SPRINGS RECREATION AREA

Trail Junction–Ski Trail

Hall Lake

Norris Rd.

Trail Junction–Ski Trail P

North Country Trail

P

2

430 Gun Lake Rd.

Hastings Point Rd.

0.3 Pass under power lines.

0.7 Join the North Country Trail.

1.0 Reach the top of Graves Hill.

1.5 Cross a footbridge just before the North Country and Hall Lake Trails split.

1.9 Arrive back at the trailhead.

3 Yankee Springs Recreation Area– Long Lake Trail

Starting and ending with an easy interpretive trail, this hike can work for small children if confined to the initial loop, or challenge stronger legs with some steep climbs at the farthest point if done entirely.

Distance: 5.6 miles out and back

Hiking time: About 3 hours

Difficulty: Moderate due to some low-grade climbs

Trail surface: Packed dirt, some boardwalks

Best season: Spring, summer, fall

Other trail users: Cross-country skiers, crossing snowmobiles

Canine compatibility: Dogs permitted on a 6-foot leash

Fees and permits: Michigan State Park Motor Vehicle Permit required for entry

Schedule: Open daily 4 a.m. to 11 p.m.

Maps: TOPO! CD: Eastern Region 4; USGS Orangeville, Bowens Mill, Middleville, Cloverdale; maps at park contact stations

Trail contact: Yankee Springs Recreation Area, 2104 South Briggs Rd., Middleville, MI 49333; (269) 795-9081; www .dnr.state.mi.us

Other: Restrooms are available in the campground near the trailhead. This park participates in the Michigan State Park Outdoor Explorer Program.

Finding the trailhead: Drive south on US 131 to exit 61 for MI 179. At the exit, turn left onto 12th Street for under 0.1 mile to reach MI 179, where you turn left (east). Go east 7.7 miles and follow the curve to the right (south) at Briggs Road. At just under a mile, turn right on State Park Drive and continue to the parking lot entrance 0.2 mile on the right. The trailhead is just to the left of the contact station there. GPS: N42 36.8037' / W85 29.4171'

The Hike

The trail hypes the Graves Hill overlook, but this is grown in during the summer, offering no view whatsoever. In reality, the rest of the trail is worth more praise, with its varied bogs, fields, pine and hardwood forests, and the nifty Sassafras interpretive trail, a 1-mile accessible loop at the beginning (and end) of this out-and-back hike. For small kids, this loop alone is perfect.

The larger hike, however, continues from the far point of the Sassafras loop on a trail that crosses Briggs Road, following a clearly marked path of packed dirt. Just past the road crossing is a picnic area to the right (south). Footbridges cross low points, and a long boardwalk passes over a boggy area. Views of Long Lake, however, are possible when the foliage is down.

Stay on the path and avoid the occasional cross paths marked with red swatches; these are snowmobile trails. At 1.8 miles the trail begins to climb earnestly and you will see a sign for ski trails C and D. Continue straight here. The North Country Trail and the park's Chief Noonday Trail join this trail at 2.2 miles. Cross a park access road soon after, pass two ski trails on the left (north), and cross another park road all within 0.2 mile. You will pass through gates at both park roads.

In just 300 feet the Hall Lake Trail joins from the right and the most strenuous climb of the hike takes you up Graves Hill. At the point where the Hall Lake Trail appears again, to your right, you go left three minutes to the top. Another extender option is the fifteen-minute hike to the Devil's Soup Bowl (see hike 2: Yankee Springs Recreation Area–Hall Lake Trail). From here turn around and retrace

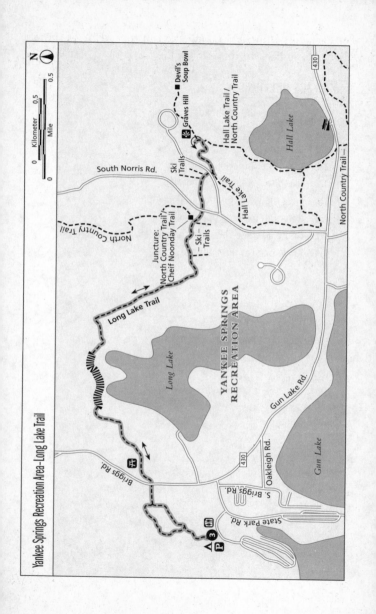

Yankee Springs Recreation Area–Long Lake Trail

your steps, ultimately taking the return branch of the Sassafras loop back to the trailhead.

Miles and Directions

0.0 Start from the trailhead.

0.4 Cross Briggs Road.

1.0 Start the long boardwalk.

2.2 Meet the North Country Trail.

2.7 Climb to the top of Graves Hill.

3.3 Pass the North Country Trail juncture again.

4.2 Return to the long boardwalk.

5.1 Go right on the Sassafras return trail.

5.6 Arrive back at the trailhead.

4 Saugatuck Dunes State Park–South Trail

This is a sometimes challenging trek along wooded dunes and out into the open dunes, with a stop at the beach along Lake Michigan.

Distance: 4.8-mile lollipop
Hiking time: About 2.5 to 3 hours
Difficulty: Easy to moderate grades, with a more challenging section in loose sand
Trail surface: Packed dirt, loose sand
Best season: Year-round
Other trail users: Cross-country skiers
Canine compatibility: Dogs permitted on leash

Fees and permits: Michigan State Park Motor Vehicle Permit required for entry
Schedule: Open daily 8 a.m. to 10 p.m.
Maps: TOPO! CD: Eastern Region 4; USGS Saugatuck; maps at park contact stations
Trail contact: Van Buren State Park, 23960 Ruggles Rd., South Haven, MI 49090; (269) 637-2788; www.dnr.state.mi.us
Special considerations: Pack water and sunscreen for the exposed areas of the dunes.

Finding the trailhead: Take I-196 west to exit 41 for Saugatuck/ Douglas. Turn right on Holland Street/Washington Road for 0.1 mile, then turn right again on 64th Street. In 0.3 mile go left on Island Lake Road, which becomes 65th Street after a slight bend to the right. Then turn left on 138th Avenue and drive 0.6 mile to the park entrance on the left (you will pass Shore Acres Drive on the left). The trailhead is to the west of the parking loop. GPS: N42 42.0188' / W86 11.7756'

The Hike

Of the two Saugatuck Dunes hikes in this book, this is the longer and more difficult. Large portions of it are shaded by hardwood forest and show ravines and ridges, which are old reclaimed dunes, but other sections are out in the open on exposed or partly grassy dunes. The climbing here is tough with the loose sand, and on a hot summer day can be extremely challenging. Carrying water with you is absolutely necessary for those stretches. The trail eventually wanders out to a long beach of Lake Michigan. Don't be distressed by some clear-cutting: The park is experimenting with strategies for the removal of invasive Austrian pine to make room for native white, red, and jack pine to repopulate the dunes.

From the parking lot, take the trail west toward the lake to a gate. Go around the gate to find the trailhead for the Livingston and South Trails. A beach trail goes up the hill to the right. This also connects to the Saugatuck Dunes State Park North Trail.

As you head south, you will pass a dead trail to private land on your left; stay on the marked path and watch for the red and blue sign. At a juncture at 0.4 mile marked point 9, go right; the path to the left goes out of the park. Another 600 feet on, the Livingston Trail is an out-and-back that goes right 0.5 mile to the beach. The South Trail continues straight.

The trail weaves among forested dunes, then crosses a park access road. The return trail will follow that road back to this point, but you continue here on the trail across the road into more ridges. At 2.3 miles you see blown-out dunes and lose the shade. The trail sand becomes loose. You'll pass

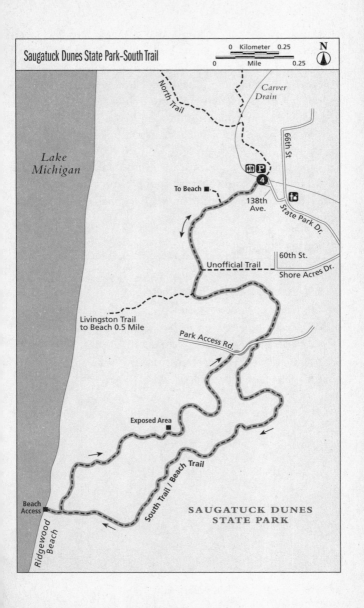

Saugatuck Dunes State Park-South Trail

0   Kilometer   0.25
0   Mile   0.25

N

North Trail

Carver Drain

66th St.

Lake Michigan

To Beach

138th Ave.

State Park Dr.

Unofficial Trail

60th St.

Shore Acres Dr.

Livingston Trail
to Beach 0.5 Mile

Park Access Rd.

Exposed Area

South Trail / Beach Trail

Beach Access

SAUGATUCK DUNES
STATE PARK

Ridgewood Beach

a 100-foot spur trail to the beach through wavelike grassy dunes. The trail starts to head back now, and you have a brief distance of tree cover before entering an area clear-cut of invasive pines. This is a strenuous climb as the trail zigzags about 0.4 mile, mostly uphill, through loose sand. Be aware of tree roots like trip wires through here.

At the top of the last climb in the open, the trail heads back into the woods on an easy path. Follow the trail to that park road you crossed earlier and then follow the road downhill to the right until it connects back to the trail on the left—the one you came in on. Backtrack to the trailhead from here.

Miles and Directions

- **0.0** Start from the trailhead.
- **0.5** Pass the Livingston Trail trailhead.
- **1.0** Cross a park access road.
- **2.5** Reach the beach.
- **3.0** Enter the clear-cut area of the dunes.
- **3.7** Go right on the park access road.
- **4.8** Arrive back at the trailhead.

5 Saugatuck Dunes State Park– North Trail

Take an easy walk through pine forest grown in over the dunes, then climb the loose sands of grassy dunes. Stop along the way for a bit of beach time and views of Lake Michigan.

Distance: 2.1-mile lollipop

Hiking time: About 1 hour

Difficulty: Mostly easy, with more challenging sections through loose sands

Trail surface: Packed dirt, loose sand

Best season: Year-round

Other trail users: Cross-country skiers

Canine compatibility: Dogs permitted on leash

Fees and permits: Michigan State Park Motor Vehicle Permit required for entry

Schedule: Open daily 8 a.m. to 10 p.m.

Maps: TOPO! CD: Eastern Region 4; USGS Saugatuck; maps at park contact stations

Trail contact: Van Buren State Park, 23960 Ruggles Rd., South Haven, MI 49090; (269) 637-2788; www.dnr.state.mi.us

Special considerations: Pack water and sunscreen for dune climbing, and use proper footwear.

Finding the trailhead: Take I-196 west to exit 41 for Saugatuck/Douglas. Turn right on Holland Street/Washington Road for 0.1 mile, then turn right again on 64th Street. In 0.3 mile go left on Island Lake Road, which becomes 65th Street after a slight bend to the right. Then turn left on 138th Avenue and drive 0.6 mile to the park entrance on the left (you will pass Shore Acres Drive on the left). The trailhead is to the north of the parking loop. GPS: N42 42.0723' / W86 11.7382'

The Hike

This book contains two Saugatuck Dunes State Park loop hikes that explore the dunes and the forest and grasses that have populated them. This is the easier and shorter of the two. The northern section of the park consists of color-coded loops: a shorter red loop embedded in the longer green loop. They overlap from the trailhead and part ways about halfway through, only to rejoin for the return. Taking the red loop as a cutoff shaves about a quarter mile off the trek.

The packed dirt trails are clearly marked and easy going, but there are portions of the trail that are simply loose sand. Take this into consideration when choosing footgear. The loose sand makes for some serious work getting up inclines, but you can expect this only just before the beach access and along the east–west crossings of both the red and green trails. Be aware of false and unofficial trails, and stay on the path to protect the fragile ecosystem.

Just beyond the trailhead, the trail loop begins at a map board. Go left and pass a connector trail to a beach trail that originates in the parking lot. There are a lot of pines through here, along with their resident woodpeckers. Continue on the red/green trail to a T juncture. To the left is a climb over the low dunes to the beach. If you want to explore the beach a bit, mark the signpost/map board to get back to the trail. (Alternatively, you could walk south along the shore to the beach trail back to the parking lot.)

Back at the T juncture on the red/green trail, continue west to a map board and a split in the trail: Red goes to the right, green goes left. Both have loose sand and a few short but steep sections, and both pass through open grassy areas

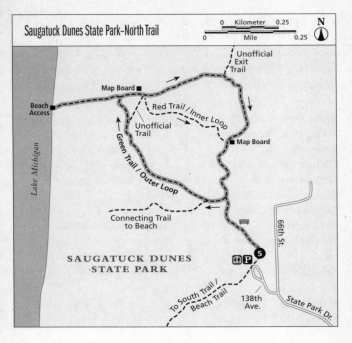

that will be hot in the summer. The inner red loop is both steeper and looser. The green trail offers a nice view back over the wide grassy area just before it rejoins the red trail (coming from the right) and continues back to the trailhead.

Miles and Directions

0.0 Start from the trailhead.

0.2 Go left at the trail juncture.

0.7 Reach the T juncture and go left to the beach.

1.2 Arrive from the beach at the red/green trail split.

1.7 From the green trail, connect back into the red trail.

2.1 Arrive back at the trailhead.

6 Millennium Park

Take a stroll through one of Grand Rapids' newest parks and see waterfowl and other birdlife on a smooth and easy path.

Distance: 4.4-mile lollipop
Hiking time: About 2 hours
Difficulty: Easy
Trail surface: Paved, gravel road
Best season: Year-round
Other trail users: Bicyclists
Canine compatibility: Dogs permitted on leash
Fees and permits: None (fee for beach use)
Schedule: Park open daily 7 a.m. to dusk
Maps: TOPO! CD: Eastern Region 4; USGS Grandville,
Grand Rapids West; map on park website
Trail contact: Kent County Parks Department, 1700 Butterworth St. SW, Grand Rapids, MI 49534; (616) 336-7375; www.access kent.com/parks
Special considerations: From Nov through Apr parking is across Maynard Avenue. The trail is exposed, so count on using sunscreen.

Finding the trailhead: Take Butterworth Street SW to Maynard Avenue SW. Turn left (south) and drive 1.1 miles to the park entrance on the right (west) side of the street. Enter the parking lot and go to the very end to the trailhead. GPS: N42 56.0501' / W85 44.9835'

The Hike

Millennium Park is one of the largest urban parks in the United States and offers 1,500 acres of recreation land that was once occupied by gravel pits and gypsum mines.

From the parking lot, venture first out onto the little boardwalk over the water to have a look at whatever waterfowl might be lurking there. Then follow the wide asphalt

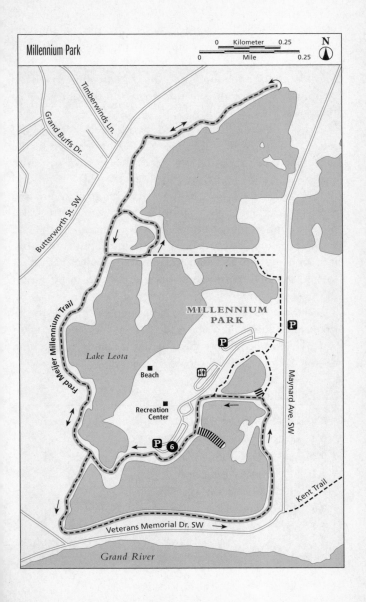

Millennium Park

0 Kilometer 0.25
0 Mile 0.25

N

Timberwinds Ln.

Grand Buffs Dr.

Butterworth St. SW

Fred Meijer Millennium Trail

Lake Leota

Beach

Recreation Center

MILLENNIUM PARK

P

P

P

6

Maynard Ave. SW

Kent Trail

Veterans Memorial Dr. SW

Grand River

path west, with water on both sides, to the first trail juncture and go right (north). The trail follows the lagoon edge, with thick forest and brush on your left. Also to the left is a creek meandering into the forest, and to the right you can see the swimming beach and recreation center on the other side of the water.

At 0.9 mile you come to a fork with a gravel trail to the left. Continue to the right instead and make a left at the next juncture. This little loop takes you north away from the pavement. At the next juncture go right (north) and follow this crushed stone road north to the park's boundary, through fields and a few random oil wells with short gravel paths leading to them from the trail. Turn around at the end and return along this path, keeping straight at junctures until it reconnects with the asphalt. Follow the asphalt path back to the very first trail juncture and go right to make a loop of the southernmost lagoon.

At the south side of the lake, the trail passes exits to the street and climbs high above the water. Descend again to water level and complete the loop of the lagoon, taking time to stop at the boardwalks to observe local wildlife.

Miles and Directions

0.0 Start from the trailhead.

0.3 Go right at the first trail juncture.

0.9 Pass a gravel road on your left.

1.1 Turn left onto a gravel path.

1.8 Reach the turnaround point.

3.0 Start the loop of the southern lagoon.

4.4 Arrive back at the trailhead.

7 North Country Trail–Lowell Area

Follow a stretch of the longest national scenic trail in America as it skirts the Flat River, strolls country back roads, and traces the tops of tree-covered ridges.

Distance: 6.5 miles one way
Hiking time: About 3 hours one way
Difficulty: Moderate for distance, surface, and climbing
Trail surface: Rustic, packed dirt
Best season: Year-round
Other trail users: None
Canine compatibility: Dogs permitted on leash
Fees and permits: None
Schedule: Open daily year-round
Maps: TOPO! CD: Eastern Region 4; USGS Lowell; maps at park office, map boards, and website

Trail contact: North Country Trail Association, 229 East Main St., Lowell, MI 49331; (866) 445-3628; www.northcountrytrail.org
Special considerations: Roadside parking is not possible at the trailhead. One-way hikers will want to leave a car at the end of the hike.
Other: Follow the blue blazes on posts and trees. The NCT is evolving, and some segments come and go with private property easements. Some portions are on country roads.

Finding the trailhead: Go east on MI 21/Fulton Street E 13.4 miles to Lowell, turning left (north) on North Hudson Street SE. This becomes Lincoln Lake Avenue. At Fallasburg Park Drive go right (east) 1.8 miles to find the trailhead on the right side of the road. GPS: N42 59.5014' / W85 19.6190'

The Hike

The North Country Trail crosses seven northern states from New York to North Dakota, a distance of over 4,600 miles,

making it the longest national scenic trail in the United States. This is a lovely segment of it not far from Grand Rapids. This Lowell segment runs north to south, often along the banks of the Flat River and over a number of forested hills and ridges before ending just north of Lowell itself. This is primarily private property, so stay on the trail and respect signage.

Starting from the trailhead, the path is strewn with stones and descends toward the river. At 0.5 mile you reach the top of a ridge with a spur down to the river, but you go right instead and hop rocks across an incoming creek. At 0.7 mile take a footbridge across the Flat River and go right on the other side through Fallasburg County Park. Pick up the trail near the edge of the river to the south end of the park clearing. At 1 mile the trail goes left (east) and takes you away from the water, and in another 0.5 mile you come out at Covered Bridge Road. Go left on the road to the next right on Montcalm Avenue. At 2.4 miles, near the top of a hill, go right to pick up the trail again at a small parking area. A map is posted here.

The trail then follows a high ridge over the river 1.2 miles to the next parking lot and Flat River Drive. Go right (west) 500 feet, cross the road, and take the trail into an open field. At the next juncture go right (west) and cross a stream at 4.2 miles. Cross Grindle Drive at 4.8 miles and pass through 0.3 mile of woods to come to Grindle again. Head straight (west) 0.3 mile along Grindle to the next bend, where the trail resumes. In 500 feet you come to a fork; go right to stay on the trail.

At 6.1 miles the trail becomes rather narrow atop a very steep ridge and heads left (west). Be cautious of the edge. Just 500 feet along is another trail juncture: Straight goes

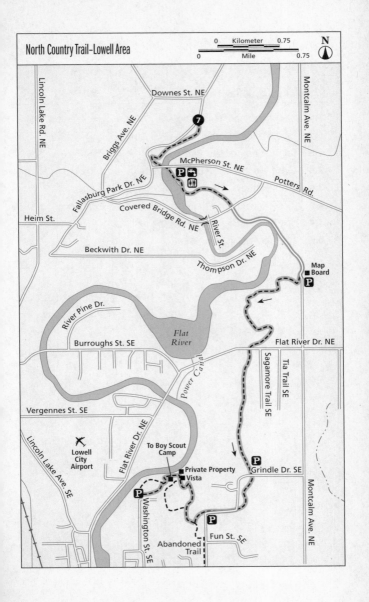

Kilometer
0   0.75

Mile
0   0.75

N

Lincoln Lake Rd. NE

Downes St. NE

Montcalm Ave. NE

Briggs Ave. NE

7

McPherson St. NE

Potters Rd.

Fallasburg Park Dr. NE

P

Covered Bridge Rd. NE

River St.

Heim St.

Beckwith Dr. NE

Thompson Dr. NE

Map Board

P

River Pine Dr.

Flat River

Flat River Dr. NE

Burroughs St. SE

Power Canal

Tia Trail SE

Sagamore Trail SE

Vergennes St. SE

Flat River Dr. NE

Lowell City Airport

To Boy Scout Camp

Private Property Vista

P

Grindle Dr. SE

Montcalm Ave. NE

Lincoln Lake Ave. SE

P

Washington St. SE

P

Fun St. SE

Abandoned Trail

to a Boy Scout camp, but you go left (south) away from the river for the final stretch through the woods to end at Washington Street.

Miles and Directions

0.0 Start from the trailhead.

0.7 Take the footbridge over the Flat River.

1.5 Turn left on Covered Bridge Road.

2.4 Leave Montcalm Avenue for the trail.

3.6 Cross Flat River Drive.

4.8 Cross Grindle Drive the first time.

5.4 Hike Grindle Drive and enter the trail.

6.5 Arrive at Washington Street.

8 Pickerel Lake

This nature preserve features a popular trail system offering options for more strenuous hill climbs or simple boardwalk passage along the lake or marshland.

Distance: 3.4-mile loop
Hiking time: About 1.5 hours
Difficulty: Easy to moderate; more challenging on Red Trail
Trail surface: Packed dirt, grass, boardwalk
Best season: Year-round
Other trail users: Cross-country skiers
Canine compatibility: Dogs not permitted
Fees and permits: None

Schedule: Open daily 7 a.m. to dusk
Maps: TOPO! CD: Eastern Region 4; USGS Cannonsburg; maps on map board and website
Trail contact: Kent County Parks Department, 1700 Butterworth St. SW, Grand Rapids, MI 49534; (616) 336-7375; www .accesskent.com/parks
Other: You might see flying squirrels here in the evening.

Finding the trailhead: From its juncture with I-196, take MI 44/ East Beltline Avenue north and stay on it as it changes road names, eventually becoming MI 44/Belding Road heading due east. Turn right (south) on Ramsdell Drive NE and drive 1 mile to the park entrance on the right (west) side. The trailhead is at the end of the parking lot. GPS: N43 4.4242' / W85 27.7610'

The Hike

Pickerel Lake, also known as the Fred Meijer Nature Preserve, has a great system of color-coded trails through varied ecosystems, and both map boards and interpretive signage are abundant. The easiest path is the 1.9-mile Lake Trail

(blue), which is a loop around the lake. The 0.9-mile Wood-land Trail (red) is the most strenuous. The selected route here combines all the trails to make a nice varied 3.4-mile loop of the entire park.

Just beyond the trailhead, go left at the first juncture. You immediately come to a wheelchair-accessible boardwalk that skirts the southern edge of the lake. Just past the end of the boardwalk is another small bridge, then arrive at a map board and restrooms to the left at 0.3 mile. The next juncture is a short alternative trail that swings closer to the lake on your right but reconnects just 200 feet farther on.

At just over 0.5 mile you reach the juncture of the wooded Sandy Knoll Trail (white). Take this trail left and it touches on the light brown Larch Swamp Trail and board-walk (next fork to the left), an alternative course for part of the white trail. Continuing south, the white trail climbs to higher ground for the return of its elongated loop over a sandy but forested knoll. Returning, you can take the brown Woodland Branch Trail to the left at 1.5 miles to connect to the red Woodland Trail at 1.6 miles and go left again. (Along the red trail is the orange Highland Trail to the left, a 0.4-mile diversion that only really adds 0.2 mile to your hike.)

The red trail reconnects to the blue Lake Trail at the lake at 2.4 miles. Go left to continue a clockwise circle of the lake. The blue trail has an observation deck, but to reach it you would need to go right here to go back 0.2 mile, if coming from the red trail. After the red trail juncture, the blue trail leaves the lakeshore and follows a more rolling terrain in the woods. You will pass old park roads up the hill from the lake and a log fence before arriving at a boardwalk at 2.9 miles and another boardwalk with a turnstile at 3.1 miles. Just past the second boardwalk is a spur trail to the

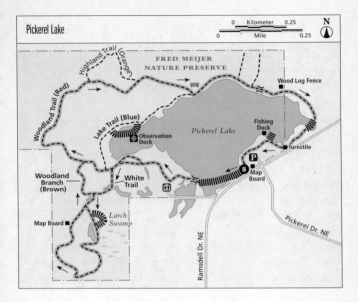

right that will take you to a fishing platform/observation deck before you arrive back at the trailhead soon after.

Miles and Directions

0.0 Start from the trailhead.

0.5 Enter the Sandy Knoll Trail.

1.5 Take the Woodland Branch Trail.

1.6 Go left on the Woodland Trail.

2.4 Connect to the Lake Trail.

2.8 Pass the log fence.

3.1 Enter the turnstile.

3.4 Arrive back at the trailhead.

9 Bass River Recreation Area

A serpentine mountain-bike path takes you through thick young woods and a section of pine where you are likely to encounter a lot of woodpeckers.

Distance: 4.4-mile loop
Hiking time: About 2 hours
Difficulty: Easy
Trail surface: Paved
Best season: Year-round
Other trail users: Mountain bikers
Canine compatibility: Dogs permitted on leash
Fees and permits: Day-use fee

Schedule: Open daily year-round
Maps: TOPO! CD: Eastern Region 4; USGS Nunica
Trail contact: Michigan Department of Natural Resources; (231) 798-3711; www.dnr.state.mi.us
Special considerations: There are no facilities here. Avoid hiking during hunting season.

Finding the trailhead: From US 31 drive 7 miles east on Lake Michigan Drive (MI 45). Take 104th Avenue north 3.4 miles and look for a gravel road on the right (east). Drive to the trailhead just before a No Motor Vehicles sign and park alongside the road. GPS: N43 1.1968' / W86 2.4441'

The Hike

Despite the name, the trails at Bass River Recreation Area don't touch on running water. This trail was designed with mountain bikers in mind. Two loops can be combined into one long hike that twists and turns through the forest. The north side of the road has fewer twists and completes a loop on the south side back near the trailhead. This is also where the second loop, completely on the south side of the road,

Bass River Recreation Area

0 Kilometer 0.15
0 Mile 0.15

N

Horse Path

Grand River

P 9 ■ Fee Box

Bass River Multi-Use Trail

Bass River Rd.

Bass River Rd.

Horse Trail

104th Ave.

BASS RIVER
RECREATION AREA

joins in. Be aware that horse paths crisscross throughout the southwestern section, and be sure to follow posted arrows and the narrow footpath to stay on course. The woods are full of birds, especially woodpeckers. The understory to the north is rather thick, except in an area of pines, while the south side is much more open, offering views deep into the woods.

Loop north from the trailhead, curling west and back again to the park road, a distance of 0.7 mile. Cross the road slightly to the right to enter the southern portion. This segment ends near the park road once more at 1.9 miles, where it also connects to the next loop. Take the left branch of

the loop and in another 0.5 mile you cross a two-rut gravel road/horse path. Go a few steps to the left on the other side to continue into the woods. (You can also use this road as a cutoff by going left back to the park road and left again, west to the trailhead.) The return path crosses the two-rut road/horse path again just 200 feet to the southwest at 3.8 miles, taking you back to the park road, where you are a short walk from the trailhead to the east (right).

Miles and Directions

0.0   Start from the trailhead.

0.7   Cross the park road.

1.9   Begin the second loop.

2.4   Cross a wide horse path/road.

3.8   Return across the wide horse path/road.

4.4   Arrive back at the trailhead.

10 Seidman Park

Three loops combine for a hike through pines whispering in the breeze, over a scenic creek, and into mixed forest and a bit of marshland.

Distance: 4.4-mile triple loop
Hiking time: About 2 hours
Difficulty: Easy
Trail surface: Packed dirt
Best season: Year-round
Other trail users: Cross-country skiers
Canine compatibility: Dogs permitted on leash
Fees and permits: None
Schedule: Open daily 7 a.m. to dusk

Maps: TOPO! CD: Eastern Region 4; USGS Cascade; map on website
Trail contact: Kent County Parks Department, 1700 Butterworth St. SW, Grand Rapids, MI 49534; (616) 336-7375; www .accesskent.com/parks
Other: Pit toilets are available at the parking lot.

Finding the trailhead: From I-96 take exit 39 for MI 21/Fulton Street going east. Drive 6 miles, just passing Pettis Avenue. Here you need to use the U-turn lane to double back to take Pettis Avenue on a slight right for just 0.3 mile. Take Honey Creek Avenue right (north) 1.6 miles before turning right on Conservation Street. The park entrance is 0.3 mile east on your left (north), and the trailhead is clearly marked in the parking lot. GPS: N42 58.796' / W85 27.962'

The Hike

Seidman Park offers lovely forest paths with some partial views of marshy areas as well as a babbling trout stream. The abundance of jack pine is a potential draw for the very rare Kirtland's warbler. The trail system consists of three

loops—South (yellow), Middle (blue/yellow), and North (red)—with connecting trails. Enter at the trailhead into a combination of towering old trees and some saplings trying to grow up between them. You will see the other trail from the lot joins you on the right just before the bridge over Honey Creek. On the other side of the bridge, go left on the main trail. (Another parallel trail on your left is closer to the creek but soon joins the main trail again.)

These are ski trails in the winter, so you will see trails that split off for short distances to accommodate skiers who prefer less of a grade at certain points. You will hit the first of these side trails at 0.3 mile and another at 0.6; take either path—they reconnect a few dozen paces farther on. At the next juncture at 0.8 mile, go left. The path to the right is your return trail.

This is the connecting trail, which also has two paths that rejoin at a boardwalk that leads to the Middle Loop. Stay left at the next juncture and again at a cutoff trail at 1.2 miles. At 1.6 miles a spur trail to the left leads to the northern parking lot, and at 1.9 miles a trail to the right is the cutoff to complete the Middle Loop. Go left instead and complete the North Loop, passing another exit trail to the northern lot to the west (left) before the trail curves east and then back south.

You'll pass the easterly ends of the cutoffs at 2.5 miles and 3 miles before coming to a short spur trail on the left to a marshy area. After viewing the marsh, backtrack to the trail and pick up the boardwalk to the left at the next juncture. After the boardwalk, stay left at the next two junctures to find your return path on the South Loop. At the next split in the trail, stay left once again and the trail brings you all the way back to the bridge at Honey Creek. Cross back over

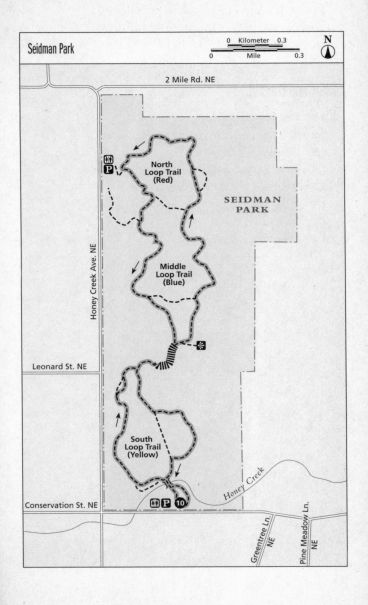

the creek and either follow the path to the left along the trout stream to get back to the parking lot or just come out the way you came in.

Miles and Directions

0.0 Start from the trailhead.

0.8 Turn left at the South Loop juncture.

0.9 Cross the boardwalk.

1.9 Go left at the North Loop juncture.

3.2 Take the spur trail for the marsh view.

3.5 At the South Loop juncture go left.

4.1 Cross Honey Creek.

4.4 Arrive back at the trailhead.

11 Rosy Mound Natural Area

Explore the amazing dunes of the Lake Michigan shoreline with well maintained steps and boardwalks as well as inter-pretive signs, beach access, and scenic overlooks.

Distance: 2.6-mile double loop
Hiking time: About 1 to 1.5 hours
Difficulty: Easy to moderate due to lots of stairs
Trail surface: Crushed limestone, boardwalks
Best season: Year-round
Other trail users: None
Canine compatibility: Dogs not permitted
Fees and permits: Day-use fee Memorial Day to Labor Day
Schedule: Open daily 7 a.m. to 10 p.m. Apr through Oct, 7 a.m. to 8 p.m. Nov through Mar

Maps: TOPO! CD: Eastern Region 4; USGS Grand Haven; maps on map board and website
Trail contact: Ottawa County Parks, 12220 Fillmore St., West Olive, MI 49460; (616) 738-4810; www.miottawa.org
Special considerations: Climbing on dunes prohibited. No fires, camping, or alcohol allowed. Wheelchair-accessible portion does not cross the dunes.
Other: Restrooms are available near the beach and the parking lot. Grills and picnic tables are near the lot.

Finding the trailhead: Take US 31 south from Grand Haven to Hayes Street and go right (west). Turn left (south) on Lakeshore Drive and the park entrance is 0.7 mile on the right (west) side. The trail-head is near the information board right in the parking lot. GPS: N43 1.2585' / W86 13.3304'

The Hike

Rosy Mound is the easiest place to see the famed Lake Michigan dunes. It's a small park with excellent boardwalks,

clear trails, and educational signage along the way. From the trailhead a wide, crushed limestone path heads into the shade of mixed forest where acorns speckle the trail. At the first juncture, marked point 2, go right; the left is your eventual final stretch on the return.

The dunes are grown over with tree cover and, closer to the lake, just grass. You immediately start a climb on wide steps. There are benches at the bottom, at the top, and a couple of places in between if you get breathless. Boardwalks cover most of the level areas. Near the top is a bench with a great overlook. The climb continues up over the highest dune, and then steps go right down to the boardwalk at the bottom. There you will find restrooms and a small trail network with three beach access points. Swimming is allowed, but there's no lifeguard. You can walk the beach to reenter the trail or follow the boardwalk along the backside of the dunes heading north. From the beach you can see the red lighthouse at Grand Haven in the distance. You can also see blowouts, where wind has managed to remove some of the protective growth, exposing the sand of the dunes.

Go north on the boardwalk to the third beach access point and you will find point 6. The beach access is to the left, but you go right on the White Pine Trail loop. At the next fork you can go in either direction—either way, you're coming back to this point. At the far end of this 0.2-mile loop is a short spur to a view of the dunes rising above you. This takes you through long-needle pines for a completely different set of sounds and smells.

Backtrack to the beach access and head left to return the way you came, all the way back up the steps. At the bottom on the backside of the dunes, just before you return to the parking lot, remember to take the path to the right, which

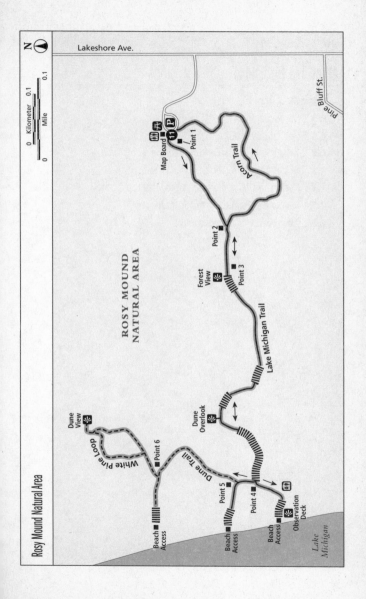

Rosy Mound Natural Area

N

Lakeshore Ave.

0 Kilometer 0.1

0 Mile 0.1

ROSY MOUND
NATURAL AREA

Map Board

Point 1

Acorn Trail

Point 2

Point 3

Forest View

Lake Michigan Trail

Dune Overlook

Dune View

White Pine Loop

Point 6

Dune Trail

Point 5

Point 4

Beach Access

Beach Access

Beach Access

Observation Deck

Lake Michigan

Pine

Bluff St.

completes the trail loop through some pine plantation near the parking lot.

Miles and Directions

0.0 Start from the trailhead.

0.3 Steps begin.

0.5 See the overlook.

0.7 Take the open stairs down to the boardwalk.

1.2 Begin the White Pine Loop.

1.8 Return to the stairs back up to the top of the dunes.

2.2 Follow the final loop to the right.

2.6 Arrive back at the trailhead.

12 Cooper Creek/Spencer Forest

Follow leaf-laden paths through a quiet forest with a place to picnic near a creek.

Distance: 3.0-mile lollipop

Hiking time: About 1.5 hours

Difficulty: Easy but uneven trail surface

Trail surface: Packed dirt, tree roots

Best season: Year-round

Other trail users: Equestrians, cross-country skiers

Canine compatibility: Dogs permitted on leash

Fees and permits: None

Schedule: Open daily year-round hours

Maps: TOPO! CD: Eastern Region 4; USGS Greenville West; map on website

Trail contact: Kent County Parks Department, 1700 Butterworth St. SW, Grand Rapids MI 49544; (616) 336-7275; www .accesskent.com

Special considerations: There are no facilities on-site.

Finding the trailhead: Take US 131 north from Grand Rapids to MI 57/14 Mile Road NE, then go east (right) 11.2 miles to Lincoln Lake Avenue NE. Go north (left) 3.2 miles and turn east (right) on 17 Mile Road NE. The parking lot entrance is on the left 1.7 miles down the road. The trailhead is on the north side of the lot. GPS: N43 13.2895' / W85 19.5940'

The Hike

This out-of-the-way county park offers a pleasant walk in the woods where you are unlikely to see other hikers but maybe the occasional horse rider. From the trailhead at the parking lot, head down a wide gravel road to a loop of gravel alongside Cooper Creek. There is a picnic table and grill

here, along with access to the edge of the water, but go to the right (east) to find the trail heading into the woods and uphill toward the road. At 0.2 mile you will pass a spur trail to the road on your right; continue on and at 0.4 mile you will cross 17 Mile Road and reenter forest on the other side slightly to the left (east).

Just 0.2 mile into the tall trees, the trail splits. Go to the right and stay on official trails. The main trail traces a rough rectangle around the park, with some less worn paths crossing through the middle. You'll pass the first of such paths on the left at 0.7 mile. Go to the right and at 0.9 mile you'll pass another. At the mile mark and 500 feet later are trails that exit the loop to the right. Go left at both, following the arrows. NO TRESPASSING signs at 1.1 miles will make this clear—there is a correctional facility beyond.

You will pass a couple more trails, one to the left that crosses the park center. At 1.5 miles you will hit a T intersection; go to the right and soon after the trail heads left (east) again. At another four-way crossing at 1.7 miles, head north (left) back toward the road. At a three-way juncture at 2.2 miles, go left (west) and follow the path back to the entry trail from the road. Exit to the road and either go all the way back to the creek on the trail you came in on across the road, or just follow the road itself west to the parking lot.

Miles and Directions

0.0 Start from the trailhead.

0.2 Enter the woods from the picnic area.

0.4 Cross 17 Mile Road.

0.6 The trail splits and you go right.

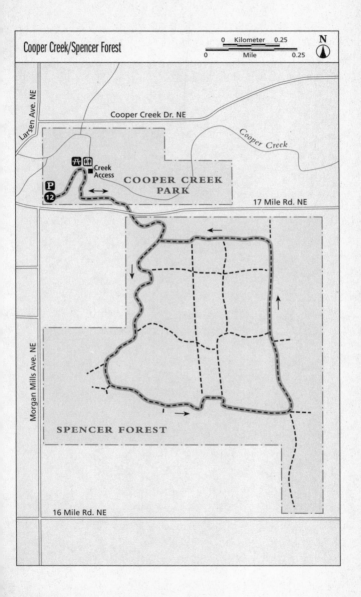

Cooper Creek/Spencer Forest

COOPER CREEK PARK

SPENCER FOREST

Larsen Ave. NE

Cooper Creek Dr. NE

Cooper Creek

Creek Access

17 Mile Rd. NE

Morgan Mills Ave. NE

16 Mile Rd. NE

0   Kilometer   0.25

0   Mile   0.25

N

P

12

1.1 Pass the first correctional facility sign.

1.7 Turn left at the southeast trail intersection.

2.7 Cross 17 Mile Road again.

3.0 Arrive back at the trailhead.

13 Aman Park

Choose from five easy short hikes through woods and marsh and over ridges bordering the meandering Sand Creek, which divides this park. Or stay longer and combine portions of all five hikes to make a big loop of the park's varied terrain.

Distance: 3.7-mile loop
Hiking time: About 1.5 hours
Difficulty: Easy
Trail surface: Packed dirt
Best season: Year-round
Other trail users: Cross-country skiers
Canine compatibility: Dogs permitted on leash
Fees and permits: None
Schedule: Open daily dawn to dusk

Maps: TOPO! CD: Eastern Region 4; USGS Grandville; map at trailhead
Trail contact: Grand Rapids Department of Parks, 201 Market Ave. SW, Grand Rapids, MI 49503; (616) 456-3696; www.grcity.us
Special considerations: There are no facilities on-site.

Finding the trailhead: Take I-196 west to exit 75 for MI 45/Lake Michigan Drive and continue west 6 miles to the park entrance on the right (north). The trailhead is at the end of the park road before it turns right to a turnaround. GPS: N42 58.6229' / W85 49.8207'

The Hike

So conveniently close to Grand Rapids, Aman Park is a 331-acre beauty with a system of trails designated by colors, some overlapping or with different lettering (A–E). Map boards make it clear where you are and give the lengths of

each trail. The terrain varies: While much of the park is level ground and mixed forest, there are marshy areas and some short climbs over low ridges that follow along the course of the central Sand Creek. Deep in the park are markers recognizing two historical figures: a monument to Edwin Sweet, a nineteenth-century settler, and the grave of Jacob Aman, who willed the land to create the park.

The main interpretive trail, red on the map boards, is a circle of the park interior, and all the trails touch or overlap it. Just a short walk from the trailhead, the overlapping orange and yellow loops split from the red and go to the right; this is also an E loop. At its turnaround point you can choose to continue on the orange (E) trail through less trodden woods or follow the yellow (A) along a ridge. Both return to the red trail, but the A loop returns to the trailhead from here.

Upon completing the orange (E) loop, take a right heading west, passing the yellow trail (A's return) on your right, and continue over a bridge on Sand Creek. The next right is the blue (C) loop, a lollipop up through marshy patches along the creek. Coming back to the red trail you will come to another juncture with the green (D) loop heading off to the right. It too returns to the red trail farther along the red's length, where you continue to where the trail ends at the park road and then walk back to the trailhead.

Miles and Directions

0.0 Start from the trailhead.

0.4 Pass Edwin Sweet's monument.

0.6 See Jacob Aman's grave.

1.0 Cross Sand Creek.

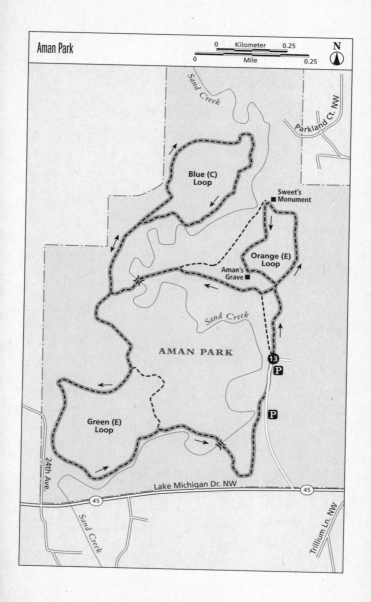

Aman Park

Blue (C) Loop

Sand Creek

Parkland Ct. NW

Sweet's Monument

Orange (E) Loop

Aman's Grave

Sand Creek

AMAN PARK

13
P

P

Green (E) Loop

24th Ave.

Lake Michigan Dr. NW

45

Sand Creek

45

Trillium Ln. NW

N

Kilometer
0   0.25

Mile
0   0.25

2.2 Complete the blue (C) loop.

2.5 Go right on the green (D) loop.

3.3 Cross the bridge over Sand Creek.

3.7 Arrive back at the trailhead.

14 Blandford Nature Center

This urban nature center offers an easy escape to someplace natural and beautiful. Walk through the woods and prairie or along wetlands, all in the space of 143 acres with educational experiences to boot.

Distance: 3.2-mile loop
Hiking time: About 1.5 hours
Difficulty: Easy
Trail surface: Cedar chips, packed dirt, boardwalks, grass
Best season: Year-round
Other trail users: None
Canine compatibility: Dogs allowed on leash on all trails but the Wilderness Trail
Fees and permits: None, except for special programs
Schedule: Trails open daily dawn to dusk. Interpretive center open Mon through Fri 9 a.m. to 5 p.m., Sat noon to 5 p.m.

Maps: TOPO! CD: Eastern Region 4; USGS Grand Rapids West; maps at park office
Trail contact: Blandford Nature Center, 715 Hillburn Ave. NW, Grand Rapids, MI 49504; (616) 735-6240; www.blandfordnaturecenter.org
Special considerations: The park gate is only open during interpretive center hours. Park outside the front gate if you plan to arrive earlier or stay longer.
Other: Restrooms and water are available at the interpretive center.

Finding the trailhead: From I-196 take exit 75 for MI 45/Lake Michigan Drive, heading west. Continue 1.6 miles west and turn right (north) on Collindale Avenue. In 1 mile take a left (west) turn onto Leonard Street. The first right is Hillburn Avenue, which takes you 0.6 mile straight into the nature center. Park in the lot. The trailhead is at the south side of the parking lot to the left of the log cabin. GPS: N42 59.7016' / W85 44.3489'

The Hike

Opened in 1968 when the Blandford family donated the land from a former farm they had purchased, this wonderful nature center has been educating the public about ecology and sustainable living ever since. The park has a nicely maintained series of connected loops that highlight different ecosystems, all in a neatly wrapped package that is accessible and manageable even for children. Trails range in length from 0.2 to 0.7 mile, but when combined in a series, make for almost 4 miles of hiking. Besides the interpretive center, educational offerings include a collection of nineteenth-century buildings brought here to highlight life back in the day.

Start left of the log cabin on the East Loop, heading south, and take it east (left) at the open field where it crosses the road and goes into the woods on cedar chips. At the next four-way juncture, go right and you are on Blue Heron Highway, with benches, boardwalks over ponds, and an observation tower along the way. Continue on the trail to the park road and cross to the other side to walk back north along the prairie and wetlands to your left. Return to the East Loop and enter the woods across the road again, this time continuing straight on the East Loop as it passes a circle of benches and crosses a bridge before taking steps down into a ravine.

On the other side the East Loop connects to the West Loop. Go left here and you can explore the Wilderness Trail, a small loop with Native American displays. Follow the West Loop to the connector for the Back Forty Loop to tackle the brushy north end of the park, where you will likely encounter deer. This loop returns to the North Farm Trail. Follow this trail to the farm, and it comes out behind

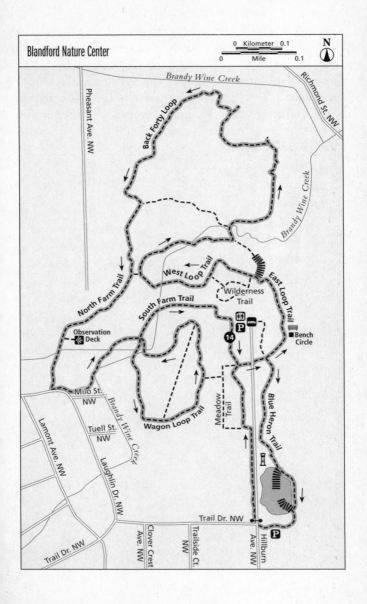

Blandford Nature Center

0 Kilometer 0.1

0 Mile 0.1

N

Brandy Wine Creek

Pheasant Ave. NW

Richmond St. NW

Back Forty Loop

Brandy Wine Creek

West Loop Trail

East Loop Trail

North Farm Trail

Wilderness Trail

South Farm Trail

Observation Deck

14

P

Bench Circle

Meadow Trail

Milo St. NW

Brandy Wine Creek

Blue Heron Trail

Wagon Loop Trail

Tuell St. NW

Laughlin Dr. NW

Lamont Ave. NW

Trail Dr. NW

Clover Crest Ave. NW

Trailside Ct. NW

Hillburn Ave. NW

P

Trail Dr. NW

Blandford School. Continue south along the woods, passing a boardwalk/observation deck, and cross a parking lot to take the South Farm Trail to the left (east) back toward the interpretive center. Just before you get to the old schoolhouse, take the Wagon Loop to the right. This will bring you back to the old village. Continue through to the parking lot.

Miles and Directions

0.0 Start from the trailhead.

0.3 Pass the observation tower.

0.9 Cross a bridge.

1.4 Go right on the Back Forty Trail.

2.3 Pass Blandford School.

2.6 Begin the Wagon Loop.

3.2 Arrive back at the trailhead.

15 P. J. Hoffmaster State Park

With its Gillette Visitor Center, the park is already worth visiting, but 3 miles of beach, dune-top overlooks of Lake Michigan, and great wildlife make this a perfect day of hiking as well as learning.

Distance: 4.1-mile loop
Hiking time: About 2 hours
Difficulty: Easy to moderate due to some strenuous dune climbs and stairs
Trail surface: Packed dirt, sand, some boardwalk
Best season: Year-round
Other trail users: None
Canine compatibility: Dogs permitted on leash
Fees and permits: Michigan State Park Motor Vehicle Permit required for entry
Schedule: Open daily 8 a.m. to 10 p.m. (unless camping in the park)

Maps: TOPO! CD: Eastern Region 4; USGS Muskegon West; maps at park office and on website
Trail contact: P. J. Hoffmaster State Park, 6585 Lake Harbor Rd., Muskegon, MI 49441; (231) 798-3711; www.dnr.state.mi.us
Special considerations: No pets or glass containers allowed on the beach. Be careful of poison ivy along the trails.
Other: Campsites with or without electricity are available, as are restrooms and water for day visitors. Visitor center hours are Tues through Sun noon to 4 p.m.; closed Mon. Call ahead to be sure.

Finding the trailhead: Take I-96 west toward Muskegon. At exit 1A turn right on Airline Road and merge with US 31, heading south toward Grand Haven. In 2.7 miles take the Pontaluna Road exit, turning right (west) toward Fruitport. Take this road 2.7 miles to its end where it curves north, becoming Lake Harbor Road. Along this curve you will see the park entrance on the left. Enter here and take the first right along that park road. This will take you into the parking area

for the beach. Watch for the trailhead on the right just before you enter the parking lot. GPS: N43 7.6369' / W86 16.2950'

The Hike

P. J. Hoffmaster is one of several Lake Michigan park beauties offering some time along the lakeshore combined with exploration of dunes that have long been reclaimed by plant life. The result is some great up-and-down trekking that often skirts the narrow ridge of a hidden dune. This hike combines the park's Walk-a-Mile Trail with a walk up the beach, a climb to observation points, and a return through the woods and past the nature center. Cross-country ski trails in other parts of the park are also options if you need more miles.

The trails show some tree roots and are often sandy. In some places—especially a few short dune climbs where there are no steps—the sand is very loose, making the going tougher. Start north on the Walk-a-Mile Trail. You will encounter a few random steps along the way and a lot of big hardwoods, until you climb over a steep dune to get to the beach and head south (with the lake on your right). Watch to your right for steps up to the cutoff trail or continue along the beach to two giant tree stumps embedded in the sand. You'll also see a sign for the visitor center.

A bit of up-and-down with stretches of boardwalk will bring you to a juncture. To the right is a trail with dirt steps, then a boardwalk out to two scenic overlooks of the lake from the top of the dunes. To the left is the end of the accessible boardwalk, which leads to an observation deck overlooking Mount Baldy, a blown-out dune. After exploring both side trails, take the straight path from this four-way juncture to the Gillette Visitor Center.

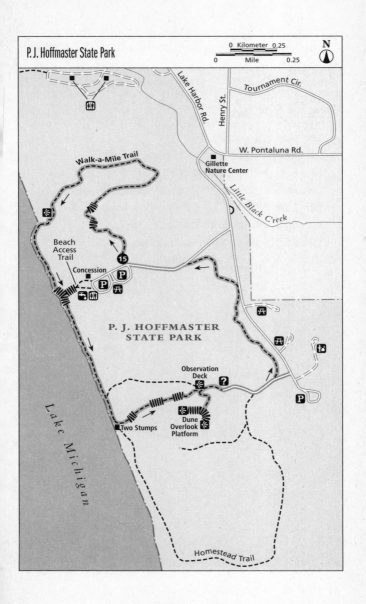

From the visitor center, follow the park road out until you see a cedar chip trail on the left (north). This will take you through the woods back to another park road, where you go left (west) 0.2 mile to return to the trailhead.

Miles and Directions

0.0 Start from the trailhead.

1.2 Reach the beach and head south.

1.5 Pass the beach access/cutoff trail.

2.0 Arrive at two giant tree stumps and enter the woods.

2.4 Explore the dune walks from the four-way juncture.

3.0 Stop at the visitor center.

3.2 Enter a cedar chip trail in the woods.

4.1 Arrive back at the trailhead.

16 Hofma Park

A crisscrossing network of skiing and hiking trails wanders this hardwood forest, giving you options to extend your hiking time without seeing the same sections of woods. The park itself has facilities for a nice outing with kids, and a nature preserve is nearby.

Distance: 3.0-mile loop
Hiking time: About 1.5 hours
Difficulty: Easy
Trail surface: Packed dirt, crushed stone
Best season: Year-round
Other trail users: Cross-country skiers
Canine compatibility: Dogs permitted on leash
Fees and permits: None

Schedule: Open daily 8 a.m. to 10 p.m.
Maps: TOPO! CD: Eastern Region 4; USGS Grand Haven; map board at trailhead
Trail contact: Grand Haven Charter Township, 13300 168th Ave., Grand Haven, MI 49417; (616) 842-5988; www.ght.org
Other: Water, restrooms, and a picnic area are on-site.

Finding the trailhead: Go west on MI 45/Lake Michigan Drive for 22 miles and turn right (north) on 144th Avenue. After 2 miles turn left (west) on Lincoln Street, then make another right (north) on 152nd Avenue 1 mile later. Take the first left onto Ferris Street and the park entrance is 0.4 mile on your right (north). Take the park road to the back of the ball diamond, where you will find the trailhead next to a sign that reads C. Reeners Nature Trail. GPS: N43 0.713' / W86 10.362'

The Hike

Hofma Park offers a network of color-coded trails through hardwood forest set amid a residential area. One could get

in a lot more than the 3 miles described here by exploring the other trails. This route gives you the opportunity to hike various parts of the woods and make cutoffs if you want to quit early. Described here is simply a loop of the park that uses the blue trail and just a bit of the red to get you to an observation deck. On the west side of the trail system is a connecting trail to Hofma Preserve, which has a few criss-crossing trails and some opportunities to see wildlife. You can reach the preserve on a trail across a long bridge, which you can't miss.

Parking is along the park road near the trailhead. From the trailhead enter the woods on a packed dirt and crushed stone trail. Just inside the woods the trail splits. Go left, following the blue trail. You will pass a trail to the playground on the left, then the yellow trail on the right before finding an intersection past a ditch. Go left (west) on the blue trail and follow it to a four-way juncture. To the left (west) you'll see the bridge to the preserve. Take the red trail north from here, keeping to the leftmost path, and you will reach a boardwalk. Take the boardwalk past an observation deck and then come back to the red trail for just a bit, continuing north to the blue. Follow the blue trail east across the park, passing the red trail to the southwest as the blue trail turns south. Continue until you arrive at a juncture where the ditch you crossed before is to your left. Follow the trail across the ditch, then continue along it to the left. Continue along this trail as it curves south and back to the trailhead.

Miles and Directions

- **0.0** Start from the trailhead.
- **0.4** Meet the yellow trail on your right.
- **1.1** Arrive at the intersection before the bridge.

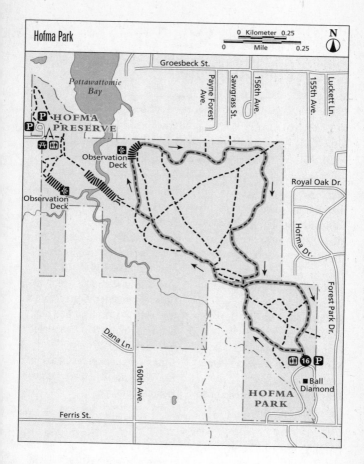

1.3 Cross the boardwalk.

2.5 Cross a ditch and head east.

3.0 Arrive back at the trailhead.

17 Muskegon State Park– Dune Ridge Trail

If the climb doesn't leave you breathless, perhaps the views of Lake Michigan and Snug Harbor from atop these dunes will. This is a challenging but beautiful trek that includes a stretch along Muskegon Lake.

Distance: 3.8-mile loop
Hiking time: About 2 hours
Difficulty: Moderate, with some more challenging dune climbs
Trail surface: Packed dirt, loose sand
Best season: Year-round
Other trail users: None
Canine compatibility: Dogs permitted on leash
Fees and permits: Michigan State Park Motor Vehicle Permit required for entry
Schedule: Open daily 8 a.m. to 10 p.m.

Maps: TOPO! CD: Eastern Region 4; USGS Muskegon West; maps at the park office
Trail contact: Muskegon State Park, 3560 Memorial Dr., North Muskegon, MI 49445; (231) 744-3480; www.dnr.state.mi.us
Special considerations: Protect yourself from the heat and sun, and wear footwear appropriate for loose sand.
Other: This park participates in the Michigan State Park Outdoor Explorer Program.

Finding the trailhead: Head west from Grand Rapids on I-96 to exit 1B for US 31 north toward Ludington. Take exit 116 on the left and continue on Business US 31 for 1 mile before taking the slight right for MI 120. After 1.1 miles turn left on Lake Avenue, then make a slight right on Center Street. Take the third left onto Ruddiman Drive, which becomes Memorial Drive. Stay on this road, though it is not straight, and follow it into the park to the lakeside Scenic Drive. Go left 1.2 miles from that intersection and find the trailhead on the

left, across from a parking area on the right. GPS: N43 13.885' / W86 20.074'

The Hike

Muskegon State Park offers some great diversity in terrain and plant life. This southern half of the park is primarily tracing sand dunes—some exposed and some covered with the slowly advancing forest and grasses. The views of Lake Michigan and Snug Harbor on Muskegon Lake are terrific, and after the hike you have a lot of Lake Michigan beach to relax on.

The first part of the hike is the most strenuous and exposed, so it is nice to start with this stretch while you are still fresh. Be prepared for climbing through loose sand with very little shade. Pay attention to wooden posts that mark the trail should drifting sand obscure the path. You will reach a dune-climb viewpoint that looks to Lake Michigan—from here you can see the red lighthouses of Muskegon. Just past this point you will pass under a big oak, but it is still open sand, with a couple of benches along the way.

When you enter the woods at 1.4 miles, the trail is firm again, and along the ridgetop you get views of the roll-ing shapes of the dunes and the lake beyond. At that first fork, go left (west) and the trail heads toward the lake on ridgetops. As the path turns north and dips east, pass an alternative crossing on your right and 0.1 mile later a spur trail up a ridge to your left. The next trail descends steeply left; take this to the bottom T juncture, which is Point B/ Devil's Kitchen. To the left are the connecting trails to the north side of the park and the Lost Lake Trail. Go right on a trail that returns east until it arrives at Muskegon Lake at Snug Harbor. Follow the trail to the right (south) along the

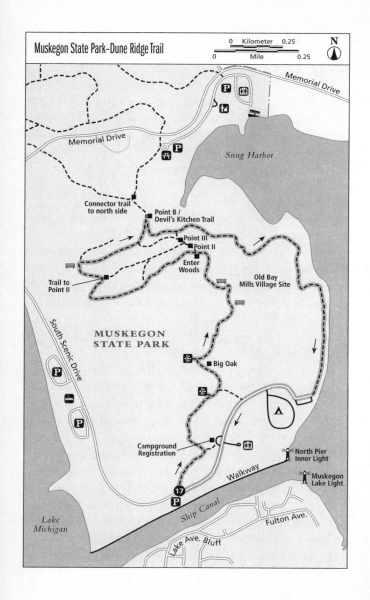

Muskegon State Park–Dune Ridge Trail

Memorial Drive

Snug Harbor

Memorial Drive

Connector trail to north side

Point B / Devil's Kitchen Trail

Point III
Point II

Enter Woods

Old Bay Mills Village Site

Trail to Point II

MUSKEGON STATE PARK

South Scenic Drive

Big Oak

Campground Registration

North Pier Inner Light

Muskegon Lake Light

Walkway

17
P

Lake Michigan

Ship Canal

Fulton Ave.

Lake Ave. Bluff

Kilometer   0   0.25
Mile   0   0.25

N

lakeshore until the path exits to the camping area. From there you must hike the park road back to where you started.

Miles and Directions

0.0 Start from the trailhead.

0.8 Pass the first bench.

1.4 Take the left branch as you enter the woods.

1.9 Go left down to Point B/Devil's Kitchen.

2.8 Arrive at the shoreline of the harbor.

3.2 Enter the asphalt park road.

3.8 Arrive back at the trailhead.

18 Muskegon State Park– Lost Lake Trail

Trace the shores of a hidden scenic lake tucked in among the rise and fall of forested dunes. This northern half of Muskegon State Park reveals hardwoods and cedars that have reclaimed the towering sands of old.

Distance: 4.2-mile lollipop

Hiking time: About 2.5 hours

Difficulty: Mostly easy, with moderate inclines

Trail surface: Packed dirt, cedar chips

Best season: Year-round

Other trail users: Cross-country skiers

Canine compatibility: Dogs permitted on leash

Fees and permits: Michigan State Park Motor Vehicle Permit required for entry

Schedule: Open daily 8 a.m. to 10 p.m.

Maps: TOPO! CD: Eastern Region 4; USGS Dalton; maps at park office

Trail contact: Muskegon State Park, 3560 Memorial Dr., North Muskegon, MI 49445; (231) 744-3480; www.dnr.state.mi.us

Other: This park participates in the Michigan State Park Outdoor Explorer Program.

Finding the trailhead: Head west from Grand Rapids on I-96 to exit 1B for US 31 north toward Ludington. Take exit 116 on the left and continue on Business US 31 for 1 mile before taking the slight right for MI 120. After 1.1 miles turn left on Lake Avenue, then make a slight right on Center Street. Take the third left onto Ruddiman Drive, which becomes Memorial Drive. Stay on this road, though it is not straight, and follow it into the park. Enter the first parking lot on your left, opposite the park office. Once inside turn left again and head east through the parking lot to find the trailhead on your left,

which leads back across the park road. GPS: N43 15.038' / W86 19.924'

The Hike

In contrast to the southern half of this park—the Muskegon State Park Dune Ridge Trail, which shows more open sand among its rows of dunes—the northern trail system is deep into thicker woods and follows a loop around an interior lake and past a luge run. You have many options as the trails crisscross throughout, but the path described here is a loop of the system.

The trail cuts through some trees from the parking lot, crosses the road, and begins along cedar chips in a marshy area with footbridges over the lowest points. The trail gets sandier as you reach the lake at 0.5 mile. Go left around the lake all the way to the northern shore, where the trail system spreads into the woods over ridges. You'll pass two connector trails up the ridge to your left marked with orange poles with XY on them, and a third with XY/XF and a yellow 12. However, your trail is the next juncture into the woods away from the lake; it forks but both paths connect to a crushed limestone trail, point 5 on the map. Head north here, following the left trail, and don't take any of the paths to the right. When you get to point 6, go left up the hill. There is an exit up steps that lead to a parking lot for the blockhouse, a small fort with a scenic overlook.

Here the trail loops back down the hill, with moderate and difficult branches for skiers down to point 8. Go straight across the four-way juncture, heading north and eventually down some steps past a luge run and on to point 1. To the left of here is the northern parking lot and sports lodge, but continue due north and then follow the trail as it curves east

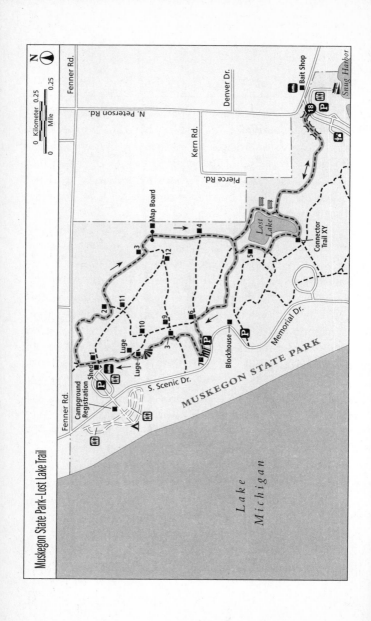

Muskegon State Park–Lost Lake Trail

N

0   Kilometer   0.25
0   Mile   0.25

Fenner Rd.
N. Peterson Rd.
Kern Rd.
Pierce Rd.
Denver Dr.

Bait Shop

Snug Harbor

18

Map Board

Lost Lake

Connector Trail XY

3
12
4
5
2
11
10
9
6
1
3
7

Luge
Luge

Shed

Campground Registration

S. Scenic Dr.

Blockhouse

Memorial Dr.

MUSKEGON STATE PARK

Lake Michigan

across the top of the park and south again for the return. At point 2 follow the trail to the left, doing so again at the next juncture and again at point 4 straight back to the lake trail, which will be on your left (southeast). Continue east around the top of the lake, completing the lake loop you started, then follow the path you came in on back to the trailhead.

Miles and Directions

0.0 Start from the trailhead.

0.5 Go left at the lakeside.

1.0 Arrive at point 5 and go left.

1.6 Come to the steps to the blockhouse.

2.2 Pass point 1.

3.3 Pass point 4.

3.7 Take the return path from the lake.

4.2 Arrive back at the trailhead.

19 Swan Creek

A rugged hike that lingers along the very edges of Swan Creek and Swan Creek Pond, this is an often overlooked trail in the Grand Rapids area offering water views and a rich woodland to explore.

Distance: 5.9-mile loop
Hiking time: About 3 hours
Difficulty: Moderate, with tricky trails along the water
Trail surface: Rustic, packed dirt, fallen trees
Best season: Spring, fall
Other trail users: None
Canine compatibility: Dogs permitted on leash
Fees and permits: None
Schedule: Open daily 4 a.m. to 11 p.m.
Maps: TOPO! CD: Eastern Region 4; USGS Millgrove

Trail contact: Allegan State Game Area Headquarters, 4590 118th Ave., Allegan, MI 49010; (616) 673-2430; www.michigan .gov/dnr
Special considerations: Count on mosquitoes, and in the summer there may be thorny creeping vines, especially on the east side of the pond. High water periods may make some parts of the trail along the water's edge impassable.

Finding the trailhead: Take US 131 south from Grand Rapids to exit 55 for MI 222. Go west (right) 9.7 miles and in Allegan take the soft right onto Monroe Street. Turn left at North Cedar Street and then right on Cutler Street, which becomes MI 40/89. Follow this road through town and turn left (west) on Monroe Road, which is also 118th Avenue. Look for the parking pull-off on the left just past Swan Creek. The trailhead is there. GPS: N42 33.0549' / W85 59.0387'

The Hike

Swan Creek and its pond are part of the Allegan State Game Area situated just a half mile east of the Department of Natural Resources (DNR) station. A yellow painted post marks the trailhead, and yellow blazes, many of which are faded and at times difficult to see, mark the trail itself. But stay with the yellow, as the ski trails are blue.

The footpath is not maintained at all and passes through mixed brush and forest. At the first junction just a few steps down the trail, go left. The path heads downhill and you overlook Swan Creek Pond. The packed dirt path is steep and tricky, with tree roots. You'll hear and see running water through here and pass some low spots that might be very soggy.

The path loops west and comes back, passing a boardwalk and bench before coming to the pond. For much of this portion of the hike, the pond is close on the left, and the trail sometimes dips right to the muddy edge. Expect a lot of fallen trees.

At 2 miles the trail climbs steeply up to a sandy lane along the top of the ridge and follows it before joining it. Follow the road out to a red gate and parking area. Cross the parking area and go left on the road, down around a curve and over the creek to the other side, where there is a sign that reads FISHING AND HUNTING ACCESS TRAIL. Go left into the woods here and the trail returns north.

You won't have much in the way of water views until you start passing the primitive campsites of Pine Point on your right, at which point there are spur trails down to the shore. Follow the trail out to the park road and go left on it. Watch for the power lines. The boat landing is down to

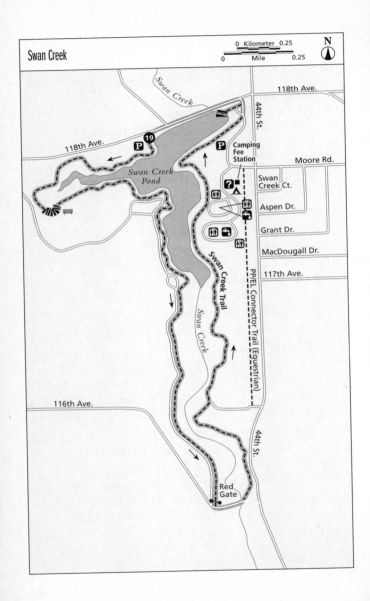

Swan Creek

0   Kilometer   0.25
0   Mile   0.25

N

118th Ave.

Swan Creek

44th St.

19   P

118th Ave.

Swan Creek Pond

P

Camping Fee Station

Moore Rd.

Swan Creek Ct.

Aspen Dr.

Grant Dr.

MacDougall Dr.

117th Ave.

Swan Creek Trail

Swan Creek

PP/EL Connector Trail (Equestrian)

116th Ave.

44th St.

Red Gate

the left. Follow the trail up along the power lines to 118th Avenue and go left (west) along the shoulder, crossing Swan Creek to get back to the trailhead.

Miles and Directions

0.0   Start from the trailhead.
0.9   Pass a boardwalk and bench.
3.0   Pass the red gate.
5.5   Reach 118th Avenue.
5.9   Arrive back at the trailhead.

20 Warren Townsend

Well suited for both walking the dog or taking the kids for a frolic, this short jaunt partly through whispering pine plantation is almost meditative as well.

Distance: 1.6-mile double loop
Hiking time: About 1 hour
Difficulty: Easy
Trail surface: Packed dirt, some asphalt
Best season: Year-round
Other trail users: Cross-country skiers
Canine compatibility: Dogs permitted on leash
Fees and permits: None
Schedule: Open daily 7 a.m. to dusk

Maps: TOPO! CD: Eastern Region 4; USGS Cannonsburg; maps on map boards and website
Trail contact: Kent County Parks, 1700 Butterworth St. SW, Grand Rapids, MI 49534; (616) 336-7275; www.accesskent.com
Other: South of 6 Mile Road across from the trailhead are complete park facilities, including restrooms and water.

Finding the trailhead: Take I-196 east toward Lansing to exit 38. Turn left (north) on MI 44/East Belt Line Avenue and continue 1.9 miles to turn right (east) on Knapp Street. Go 6 miles to Honey Creek Avenue and turn left. After 3.1 miles turn right on Cannonsburg Road and take the first left on Ramsdell Drive. In 0.3 mile turn right on 6 Mile Road and the park entrance is 0.2 mile east on your left. The trailhead is in the lot. GPS: N43 3.4609' / W85 27.6658'

The Hike

This is a fine bit of quiet time in the forest that doesn't require a lot of navigation. There are two loops, one embedded in the other: The Red Pine Trail, which is red on the

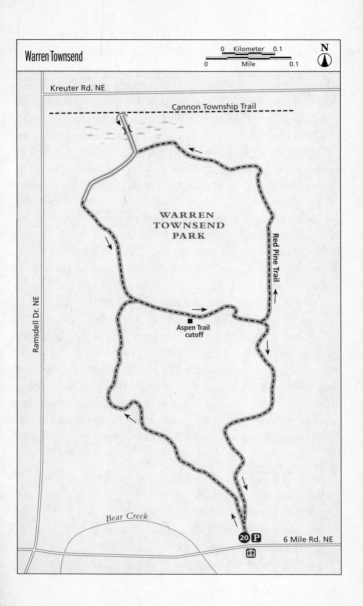

Warren Townsend

0   Kilometer   0.1

0   Mile   0.1

N

Kreuter Rd. NE

Cannon Township Trail

WARREN
TOWNSEND
PARK

Red Pine Trail

Aspen Trail
cutoff

Ramsdell Dr. NE

Bear Creek

6 Mile Rd. NE

20 P

map boards, circles the entire park and takes about an hour to complete. The Aspen Trail, which is yellow on the map boards, overlaps the Red Pine Trail but then creates a cutoff about midway through and returns along the larger trail to the trailhead. The Aspen is about half the length and time. As described here, the route is hiked as a figure eight.

From the trailhead and parking lot, climb a few steps and then start through pine plantation to a Y juncture. Go left; the right is your return path. While there are young maples in the understory, the pines, rustling softly in the slightest breeze, dominate. The trail rolls gently, with sandy patches and a carpeting of pine needles, and the woods gradually thicken with brush. The first juncture is the yellow-coded Aspen Trail to your right at 0.4 mile. The connection between the two sides of the park's loop trail is only about 800 feet. Crossing from west to east is a moderate climb and the most work you'll do here.

At the opposite end, go left (north) to make a figure eight. The northern half of the trail rises gently to the turnaround point and is downhill on the way back. At 0.9 mile you come to that turnaround, a spur trail on a bridge over swampland out to the Cannon Township Non-Motorized Trail network, a double-wide asphalt path. Continue back on the red trail, which for a few hundred feet is still asphalt, through the woods until you arrive again at the yellow trail. Cut across on the same 800-foot path and head right (south) to return to the trailhead.

Miles and Directions

0.0 Start from the trailhead.

0.4 Go right on the yellow trail.

0.9 Arrive at the bridge.

1.2 Return to the yellow trail.

1.6 Arrive back at the trailhead.

About the Author

Kevin Revolinski has written for the *New York Times* and *Chicago Tribune*, and he is the author of several guidebooks, including *Best Easy Day Hikes Milwaukee*, *Best Rail Trails Wisconsin*, *Backroads and Byways of Wisconsin*, *Wisconsin's Best Beer Guide: A Road-trip Manual*, *Michigan's Best Beer Guide*, and *The Yogurt Man Cometh: Tales of an American Teacher in Turkey*. He travels the world but makes base camp in Madison, Wisconsin. Check out his website at www.The-MadTravelerOnline.com and travel blog at Revtravel.com.

AMERICAN HIKING SOCIETY

Because you
hike.

We're with you
every step of the way

American Hiking Society gives voice to the more than 75 million Americans who hike and is the only national organization that promotes and protects foot trails, the natural areas that surround them, and the hiking experience. Our work is inspiring and challenging, and is built on three pillars:

Volunteerism and Stewardship

We organize and coordinate nationally recognized programs—including Volunteer Vacations, National Trails Day ®, and the National Trails Fund—that help keep our trails open, safe, and enjoyable.

Policy and Advocacy

We work with Congress and federal agencies to ensure funding for trails, the preservation of natural areas, and the protection of the hiking experience.

Outreach and Education

We expand and support the national constituency of hikers through outreach and education as well as partnerships with other recreation and conservation organizations.

Join us in our efforts. Become an American Hiking Society member today!

American
Hiking
Society

1422 Fenwick Lane · Silver Spring, MD 20910 · (800) 972-8608
www.AmericanHiking.org · info@AmericanHiking.org